PRESIDENTS *and* FIRST LADIES

JOHN & ABIGAIL
ADAMS

By

Ruth Ashby

WORLD ALMANAC® LIBRARY

Please visit our web site at: www.worldalmanaclibrary.com
For a free color catalog describing World Almanac® Library's list of high-quality books
and multimedia programs, call 1-800-848-2928 (USA) or 1-800-387-3178 (Canada).
World Almanac® Library's fax: (414) 332-3567.

Library of Congress Cataloging-in-Publication Data

Ashby, Ruth.
    John & Abigail Adams / by Ruth Ashby.
      p. cm — (Presidents and first ladies)
    Includes bibliographical references and index.
    ISBN 0-8368-5755-0 (lib. bdg.)
    ISBN 0-8368-5761-5 (softcover)
    1. Adams, John, 1735-1826—Juvenile literature. 2. Adams, Abigail, 1744-1818—Juvenile
literature. 3. Presidents—United States—Biography—Juvenile literature. 4. Presidents' spouses—
United States—Biography—Juvenile literature. 5. Married people—United States—Biography—
Juvenile literature. I. Title: John and Abigail Adams. II. Title.
E322.A84   2005
973.4'4'0922—dc22
[B]   2004057737

First published in 2005 by
World Almanac® Library
330 West Olive Street, Suite 100
Milwaukee, WI 53132 USA

Copyright © 2005 by Byron Preiss Visual Publications, Inc.

Produced by Byron Preiss Visual Publications, Inc.
Project Editor: Kelly Smith
Photo Researcher: Bill White
Designed by Four Lakes Colorgraphics Inc.
World Almanac® Library editorial direction: Mark J. Sachner
World Almanac® Library editor: Jenette Donovan Guntly
World Almanac® Library art direction: Tammy West
World Almanac® Library graphic designer: Melissa Valuch
World Almanac® Library production: Jessica Morris

Photo Credits:
Corbis: 7; Courtesy of Adams National Historical Park/National Park Services: 4 (bottom); Courtesy of the
Massachusetts Historical Society: 5, 8 (top), 11, 21, 27; HistoryPictures.com: 4 (top), 6, 8 (bottom), 10, 12,
13 (bottom), 15, 20, 30, 32, 34, 36, 39, 41, 42; Howard Pyle: 29; Library of Congress: 13 (top), 14, 16, 19,
22, 24, 25, 35, 38; National Archives and Records Administration: 28; National Portrait Gallery, Smithsonian
Institution: 26; Painting by Don Troiani, www.historicalartprints.com: 17
Cover art: Courtesy of Massachusetts Historical Society

Printed in Canada

1 2 3 4 5 6 7 8 9 09 08 07 06 05

CONTENTS

Words that appear in the glossary are printed in
boldface type the first time they occur in the text.

★INTRODUCTION ★ ★ ★ ★ ★ ★ ★ ★ ★

On July 1, 1774, the thirteen colonies were in turmoil. In revenge for the Boston Tea Party, Great Britain had imposed a series of harsh measures on the stubborn colonists. **Delegates**, representing each of the colonies, decided to call a general meeting, the First **Continental Congress**, in Philadelphia to determine what to do. One of the delegates was a thirty-eight-year-old lawyer from Massachusetts named John Adams. He and his wife, Abigail, had been at the center of the colonial protest from the beginning. As he was about to set off for Philadelphia, John wrote Abigail a letter asking for her support in the looming conflict with Great Britain. "I must intreat you, my dear partner in all the joys and Sorrows, Prosperity and Adversity of my Life, to take a Part with me in the Struggle."

John Adams, the second president of the United States, in a painting by Elaphilet Frazer Andrews, 1881, based on a Gilbert Stuart portrait.

Abigail did. As John and Abigail Adams devoted their lives to the cause of independence, their love and commitment endured, nurtured by mutual admiration and respect. Together, they forged one of the most remarkable partnerships in American history—and helped create a revolution.

First Lady Abigail Adams in a painting based on a Gilbert Stuart portrait from 1812.

YANKEE LAWYER

John Adams liked to say he came from a "line of virtuous, independent New England farmers." His **Puritan** ancestors, who first arrived from England in 1638, had settled in Braintree, Massachusetts, just south of Boston. Four generations later, John's father, also named John Adams, was still living there, growing wheat and corn in the rocky New England soil and serving his community as **militia** officer, town officer, and church deacon. Deacon Adams, John said, was "the honestest man" he ever knew. His mother, Susanna Boylston, was a hardworking woman with a fiery temper.

Drawing of the birthplace of John Adams by Eliza Susan Quincy, 1822.

John was born on October 30, 1735, the eldest of three sons. He grew up in a sturdy five-room **saltbox** house with a steep roof, one of a pair of houses that adjoined each other on the family homestead. He would live in one house or the other for much of his life.

John later remembered his childhood as a happy time "of making and sailing boats . . . swimming, skating, flying kites and shooting marbles," and "running about to quiltings and frolics and dances among the boys and girls." He began his schooling at a nearby **dame school,** where he learned his ABCs from *The New England Primer*. Later, he began attending a local Latin school. Although Deacon Adams was not formally educated himself, he had decided that his bright eldest son was destined for Harvard College in nearby Boston. To qualify for Harvard, John first needed a thorough grounding in classical Latin and Greek, requirements for any kind of profession in colonial New England.

In his new school, John was bored by both the teacher and the course of study. He told his father that he would rather be a farmer.

The Harvard campus where Adams spent his college years seen here in 1725.

"A farmer!" Deacon Adams said. "Well I will show you what it is to be a farmer."

The next day, John set off with his father to cut thatch in a nearby marsh. After a long, exhausting day, John still insisted that he liked farming very much.

"Ay, but I don't like it so well," Deacon Adams retorted. "You will go back to school today." And so John did, but this time to a different school, with a teacher he admired. At age fifteen, he passed his entrance examinations for Harvard. For a book lover like John, college was "total and complete happiness," he remembered later. "I read forever."

Choosing a Career

John's college years flew by, and in 1755, he was faced with the prospect of making a living—and making a name for himself. His father wanted him to study for the clergy, but John felt no call to the religious life. Still less did he want to be one of the "common herd of Mankind, who are to be born and eat and sleep and die, and be forgotten," as he wrote in his diary. No, John would be a lawyer, and "gain a Reputation." Yet, he wondered, "How shall I spread an Opinion of myself as a Lawyer of distinguished Genius, Learning, and Virtue?"

While he decided what path to take, John accepted a job as a schoolmaster in Worcester, Massachusetts. He disliked teaching immediately. Everywhere he was surrounded by a "large number of little runtlings," he grumbled, "just capable of lisping ABC and troubling the master." He was dissatisfied with his students and with himself. "I have no books, no time, no friends. I must therefore be contented to live and die an ignorant, obscure fellow."

Finally John made up his mind to study law under the guidance of a Worcester attorney. In 1758, he was admitted to practice trial law in Massachusetts. He took his first case and promptly lost it. He had been caught unprepared and vowed it would never happen again.

Although he now had a profession, twenty-three-year-old John Adams was still tormented by self-doubt. "Why have I no genius to start some new thought?" he asked himself. "Some thing that will surprise the world."

It was about that time that John first went with his friend Richard Cranch to visit the parsonage of Reverend William Smith in nearby Weymouth. Smith had two eligible teenage daughters, Mary and Abigail, but John was not taken with them. Yes, they were intelligent, he recognized, but they were "not fond, not frank, not candid."

It was not a promising introduction to the love of his life.

The Thirteen Colonies

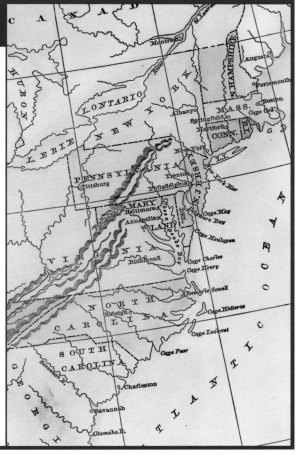

When John Adams was a boy, thirteen English colonies stretched along the Atlantic coast of North America. From north to south they were: Massachusetts (including present-day Maine), New Hampshire, Rhode Island, Connecticut, New York, Pennsylvania, New Jersey, Delaware, Maryland, Virginia, North Carolina, South Carolina, and Georgia. Altogether, about one million colonists and a half-million enslaved Africans lived there. The colonies had their own colonial governments, with governors and elected assemblies. Although they thought of themselves as loyal subjects of the British crown, colonists developed a unique American culture quite different from that of the mother country. Forty-one years after Adams was born, the colonists' independent spirit led them to break away and form their own nation.

A map of the thirteen English colonies before the American Revolution.

CHAPTER TWO

A BOOKISH YOUNG LADY

Abigail Smith was born on November 22, 1744, in the seacoast town of Weymouth, Massachusetts, where her father, William Smith, served as the local minister. Reverend Smith was a gentle scholar who loved books and kept a fine library in his home. Abigail's mother, Elizabeth Quincy Smith, ran the household, looked after her four children, and tended to the sick and needy in the parish. She taught her daughters, Mary, Abigail, and Elizabeth, and her son, William, to always be kind and considerate to others. "We should never wait to be requested to do a kind office [or] an act of love," she advised them.

Abigail Adams's birthplace, Weymouth, Massachusetts, unsigned drawing, c. 1800.

Little Abby—pale, slender, and high-spirited—was often sick and in bed. She did not mind too much, however, for being alone gave her the chance to do what she loved most, read. Her appetite for stories was first whetted by her Grandmother Quincy, who frequently read aloud to her. Later, Abigail was allowed to explore her father's library, where she pored over books on history, biography, and religion; plays by William Shakespeare; and the poetry of Alexander Pope. Reverend Smith, recognizing that his daughter had been blessed with a fine and inquisitive mind, encouraged her to develop it.

Abigail's father did not, however, offer her a more formal education, although Abby begged to be allowed to go to the local school, like her younger brother, William. Elizabeth Smith was afraid her girls, especially the fragile

Portrait of a teenage Abigail, daughter of William Smith and Elizabeth Quincy Smith.

Abigail, might become ill from contact with the other children. As a result, all her life Abigail would be self-conscious about her spelling, punctuation, and handwriting. Many years later, she would write disapprovingly, "Every assistance and advantage which can be procured is afforded to the Sons, whilst the daughters are wholly neglected in point of Literature."

When Abby was a teenager, she had the chance to spend some time at her aunt and uncle's house in nearby Boston. There she made new friends her own age with whom she kept up a lively correspondence upon her return to Weymouth. Letter writing gave her the chance to polish her writing skills and clarify her thoughts. Some of Abigail's models were the epistolary novels (written as a series of letters between the characters) of British writer Samuel Richardson. Novels were a new art form in the early 1700s. *Pamela*, a favorite of Abigail's, was a runaway bestseller in both Great Britain and America.

The Reverend Smith and his library attracted a number of educated young men who came to converse with him and with his attractive, intelligent daughters. Yet Abigail herself found few suitors, as she wrote her cousin. "Why, I believe you think they [suitable young men] are as plenty as herrings, when, alas! There is as great a scarcity of them as there is of justice, honesty, prudence, and many other virtues."

When she wrote this letter, fifteen-year-old Abigail had already met the short and stout John Adams. Apparently, like the other young men visiting her household, he had not made much of an impression on her. Soon, though, that would change.

Colonial Women in New England

In the 1700s, the primary role of New England women was to take care of their homes and families. Usually married in their late teens, many women gave birth to seven or more children and spent most of their adult lives either pregnant or recovering from pregnancy. From dawn to dusk, they cooked, cleaned, sewed, raised livestock, and tended their gardens. In the towns, some women learned trades from their fathers or husbands and became shoemakers, silversmiths, or printers. Some wives even took over their husbands' businesses when they died.

Most women had little education. "Female education in the best families went no farther than writing and arithmetic and in some few rare instances music and dancing," Abigail Adams wrote. Not until the nineteenth century would the formal schooling that Abigail craved become regularly available to the daughters of the middle class.

CHAPTER THREE

FRIENDS AND LOVERS

Two years after their initial meeting, Abigail and John met again. Now seventeen, Abigail had developed into a lovely, slender girl with a pale, delicate complexion and lively, dark eyes. At 5 feet 7 inches (about 170 centimeters), she was almost as tall as John. She found the young lawyer brilliant, talkative, and honest, every bit her match in both intellect and wit. To his diary, John confided that Abigail was "a constant feast . . . prudent, modest, delicate, soft, sensible, obliging, active."

Portrait of John after a painting by John Singleton Copley, c. 1783.

As a lawyer trying to build his reputation, John spent a lot of time on the road, traveling a circuit from one courthouse to the next. As a result, the courtship of John and Abigail was largely carried out by letters. Their letters marked the beginning of a lifelong correspondence that would bind them together even when they were forced to be apart.

John addressed her as "Miss Adorable"; she called him "My Dearest Friend." Soon they adopted classical names. Abigail signed herself "Diana," after the goddess of the Moon. He was "Lysander," a Spartan admiral. Their letters were sprightly, comfortable, and very affectionate. She owed him many kisses, John said at one point, "as I have given two or three Million at least."

In the fall of 1763, a **smallpox** epidemic hit Boston, and John decided to be inoculated. It was a difficult decision, as he ran the chance of becoming gravely ill. It was with a heavy heart that he left for Boston, where he would remain in **quarantine** for five weeks. John wrote Abigail constantly, ending one missive with the tender, "I am . . . and forever after will be your admirer and friend, and lover, John Adams."

Their courtship was not all moonlight and roses, however. John, who had always been so critical of himself, could not resist turning his searchlight on her. Abigail played cards badly, he informed her in a "Catalogue of Your Faults." He also pointed out that she couldn't sing; she slouched when she sat, an unfortunate consequence of a "Habit of Reading, Writing, and Thinking"; she sat with her legs crossed, which "Ruins the figure. . . . and injures the Health"; and she walked with her toes turned inward, like a parrot.

Abigail took his faultfinding in good humor. John should be glad she did not try to sing, she retorted, as she had a "voice harsh as the screech of a peacock." Besides, she added huffily, "a gentleman has no business to concern himself about the Leggs of a Lady."

Finally John recovered from the inoculation, and the wedding plans could proceed. As the great day approached, Abigail had her belongings shipped by cart to the Adams house in Braintree. "And—then Sir if you please you may take me," she wrote John archly. On October 25, 1764, nineteen-year-old Abigail and twenty-nine-year-old John were married.

Abigail Adams, two years after her marriage to John, in a pastel drawing by Benjamin Blyth.

Becoming a Family

The new couple settled into the old clapboard house right next to his mother's, which John had inherited when his father died in 1761. Nine months later, Abigail gave birth to their first child, a healthy daughter who was also christened Abigail but was always called Nabby. Her daughter was, Abigail wrote, "the dear image of her still dearer papa." Two years later, Nabby was followed by a brother, John Quincy, who was named after his maternal great-grandfather, and then by a sister, Susanna, in 1768.

John Adams continued to be away on business. As she was to do for much of their life together, Abigail stayed at home to manage the family and farm herself. From daybreak to sunset, she cooked, baked, cleaned, sewed her family's clothes, and churned its butter. She was the one who directed the workers on the farm, saw to the feeding and care of the livestock, and handled the family's finances.

Boston in the 1760s in an engraving by J. Carwitham. By 1768 the Adams family had moved to the busy port city.

By 1768, John was in Boston so much of the time that they decided to move the whole family there together. Abigail enjoyed the bustling city of 16,000 people, where she had merely to go down the street to shop or visit friends. For his part, John became the busiest and most successful attorney in the city, as well as a spokesman for colonial rights. Boston in the 1760s was a hotbed of unrest against Great Britain. As protests against Britain grew, the Adams family found itself in the very center of the storm.

Taxes and Tea

The problem was taxes. For nine years, Britain had carried out a war against France on American soil that had plunged Britain deeply into debt. After the French and Indian War ended in 1763, the British **Parliament** decided to tax Americans to help pay for the cost of the war. It passed the Stamp Act, which placed a tax on paper goods such as newspapers, legal documents, and playing cards. The colonial reaction was immediate. This was taxation without representation, colonists insisted. John Adams added his voice to the rising opposition. In an essay printed in the *Boston*

Gazette, he declared, "We have always understood it to be a grand and fundamental principle of the [English] **constitution** that no freeman should be subject to any tax to which he has not given his own consent."

Shocked by the resistance, Parliament repealed the law. Bostonians were not placated, however. John's cousin Samuel Adams founded a patriot group called the Sons of Liberty to protest British policies.

The year 1770 was one of the most difficult of John and Abigail's life. On February 4, their thirteen-month-old daughter, Susanna, died. They were so upset that neither of them spoke or wrote about the death for years. Just after Susanna's death, another child, Charles, was born, followed in September 1772 by a third son, Thomas Boylston.

This cartoon from 1774 displays all the ways in which British authority is being challenged by angry colonists. In the foreground, a tax collector is tarred and feathered and forced to drink tea. On the tree trunk, the Stamp Act is disgracefully hung upside down, and the Boston Tea Party takes place to the left.

Samuel Adams, John's cousin, founded a well-organized band of disgruntled Bostonians called the Sons of Liberty to protest unjust British policies. Engraving based on a portrait by John Singleton Copley.

The tension in Boston continued to escalate. On March 5, 1770, a mob outside the Boston Custom House started taunting the British soldiers on guard. As the crowd grew, it threw snowballs, oyster shells, and stones at the red-coated guards. "Lobsters!" they shouted. "Bloodybacks!" Alarmed and confused, the soldiers opened fire upon the crowd, killing five people. Immediately Sam Adams denounced what he called the "Boston Massacre."

The British soldiers were arrested, and the very next day John Adams was asked to defend them in a Massachusetts court. He promptly agreed. Though his act was deeply unpopular, Adams believed strongly that in

Paul Revere's engraving of the Boston Massacre depicts British troops opening fire on colonial protestors. In fact, the British officer, Captain Thomas Preston, never gave the order to shoot. Revere altered the facts for propaganda purposes.

a free country all accused had the right to legal counsel and a fair trial. He put up a strong argument, declaring that the soldiers were provoked by the mob and had shot in self-defense. The British soldiers were let off with only minor punishment. Ever afterward, Adams regarded the case as "one of the best services I ever rendered my country."

Boston subsided into an uneasy calm. The British had repealed most of the hated taxes on the colonies. Yet in a symbolic gesture, they retained just one—the tax on tea. An immensely popular drink, tea was imported by the English East India Company and sold to colonial merchants. Patriotic colonists, led by the Sons and Daughters of Liberty, urged colonists to **boycott** the imports. Abigail and other housewives began to serve coffee or brew "liberty tea" from strawberry, sassafras, or raspberry leaves. The effort, she wrote, made her feel very "heroic."

In early 1773, Parliament passed a law that would allow the East India Company to bypass the merchants and sell directly to the colonists. By doing so, Parliament hoped the colonists would buy the cheaper tea, even though it would still be taxed. In November 1773, three East India Company ships arrived in Boston Harbor carrying a cargo of tea. Angry citizens, determined not to pay the tax, requested that the ships leave at once. When Governor Thomas Hutchinson insisted the tea be paid for and unloaded, the Sons of Liberty were ready. The night of December 16, more than fifty men and boys disguised as Native American Mohawks boarded the ships and dumped 342 chests—more than 46 tons (41 metric tons) of tea leaves—into the harbor. John Adams, away from Boston on business, declared the Boston Tea Party a "magnificent movement," an "Epocha in history."

Abigail wrote her friend Mercy Otis Warren, "The flame is kindled and like Lightning it catches from Soul to Soul."

Great Britain retaliated at once. In a series of harsh measures, the British Parliament forbade town meetings throughout the colonies, required Boston citizens to house British troops in their homes, and most devastating of all, closed the port of Boston. **Martial law** was declared, and eleven British regiments occupied the city.

In protest against the 1773 British tax on tea, angry colonists dressed as Mohawk Indians boarded merchant ships and dumped 342 chests of imported British tea into the harbor, in an incident now known as the Boston Tea Party. Lithograph by Sarony & Major, 1846.

The Stage of Action

Throughout the thirteen colonies, citizens rallied in Boston's defense, denouncing the "intolerable acts" by the British government and shipping food to the embattled city. In addition, colonial leaders called for a meeting to decide how to respond to Parliament. All colonies except Georgia made plans to send its delegates to Philadelphia to attend the First Continental Congress.

John Adams was elected as one of five delegates from Massachusetts. "Swim or sink, live or die, survive or perish, [I] am with my country," he wrote an old friend who remained a British

John Adams, Gouverneur Morris, Alexander Hamilton, and Thomas Jefferson were colonial delegates to the First Continental Congress that gathered in Philadelphia to discuss how to respond to actions by the British Parliament. By A. Tholey, 1894.

Loyalist. "You may depend upon it." In the service of that country, he would leave his business and family in Abigail's capable hands and travel far from home. Early in 1773, he had bought the rest of his father's homestead from his brother Peter, who had inherited the other half of the family's two houses. Now John owned 35 acres (about 14 hectares) of property in Braintree and an additional 18 acres (about 7 ha) of land nearby. When they realized that John would be leaving, Abigail and the four children moved back to Braintree.

John understood the burden he was placing on his wife but trusted she would be equal to the task. "I intreat you to rouse your whole Attention to the Family, the stock, the Farm, the Dairy," he wrote her on July 1, 1774. "Let every Article of Expence which can possibly be spared be retrench'd."

Abigail gave him her complete support. "I long impatiently to have you upon the Stage of action," she confessed. On August 10, John Adams and the other delegates set out for Philadelphia.

A Patriotic Friendship

In 1773, Abigail gained a new friend in Mercy Otis Warren, essayist, poet, and playwright. Wife of Boston revolutionary James Warren, Mercy used her pen to poke fun at the British and stir up resistance to colonial rule. As the tensions between the colonies and Great Britain increased, Abigail and Mercy corresponded frequently, exchanging news and political opinions. "Is it not better to die as the last of British freemen than live the first of British Slaves?" Abigail wrote to Mercy defiantly in 1775. In the coming years, Mercy would console Abigail on John's frequent absences. "If your dearest friend had not abilities to render such important services to his country," Mercy reminded her, "he would not be called. . . ."

The friendship suffered a setback in 1806 when Mercy Otis Warren criticized John in her three-volume history of the American Revolution. However, the old friends reconciled again before Abigail's death in 1818.

REVOLUTION!

For much of the next ten years, John and Abigail would live apart, in different towns and even on different continents. They kept in touch through letters. They knew they were making history and that their letters were important. John even instructed his wife to save them. "They may exhibit to our posterity," he wrote her, "a kind of picture of the manners, opinions, and principles of these times of perplexity, danger, and distress."

The Battle of Lexington and Concord, painted by Don Troiani. The battle was the first test of American resolve and courage against trained British troops.

John wrote home about all the new sights and people he was seeing on his first trip away from New England. The Continental Congress, he wrote, was most impressive.

"There is in the Congress a Collection of the greatest Men upon this Continent, in Point of Abilities, Virtues, and Fortunes," he wrote. A month later, he was less optimistic, complaining, "The Business of the Congress is tedious, beyond Expression."

The Congress suggested a boycott of all British imports and the raising of individual militias by each colony. The Congress was in session only until October 26, 1774, and decided to meet again the next spring. John turned around and made the long trip home.

Citizens known as **minutemen** began to train throughout Massachusetts. That winter, violent confrontation with the British Army appeared inevitable. "It seems to me now the Sword is now our only, dreadful alternative," Abigail wrote Mercy Otis Warren. In Boston, the British **garrison** was increased to four thousand troops. The city was a powder keg ready to explode. In April 1775, it did.

To Arms!

British commander general Thomas Gage had learned that the minutemen kept a large store of arms in the nearby town of Concord, and he dispatched seven hundred troops to capture it. On April 19, the redcoats were met by seventy minutemen on the Lexington village green. Someone—no one knows who—fired "the shot heard round the world," and a skirmish broke out. The Revolutionary War had begun.

A few days later, John Adams left for Philadelphia and the Second Continental Congress. Although blood had already been shed, most delegates still did not want a permanent split with Great Britain. They decided to send King George III one last plea, the Olive Branch Petition, asking him to repeal the "intolerable acts." However, some delegates, Sam and John Adams among them, realized the time for peace had passed. They persuaded the others that the Congress had to establish a Continental Army to defend against the British Army now encamped in Boston. John rose to propose a commander. "I [have] in my mind," he said, "a gentleman whose skill and experience as an officer . . . whose excellent universal character would command the [approval] of all America." He was speaking, of course, of George Washington.

Meanwhile, from their home in Braintree, Abigail kept her husband up to date on the worsening situation in Boston. Though not in the city herself, Abigail had friends and family who were, and she acquired a steady stream of information from refugees and soldiers who passed through Braintree regularly. When American soldiers fortified Bunker Hill, across the Charles River from Boston, British general William Howe dispatched troops to take it back. On June 17, 1775, Abigail was awakened by the sound of cannon fire. With seven-year-old Johnny, she hastened up Penn's Hill to peer 10 miles (about 16 km) across the bay to Charlestown. It was smoldering, burned to the ground by British troops. "How many have fallen we know not," she wrote. "The constant roar of the cannon is so distressing that we cannot eat, drink, or sleep."

At first, she wrote John, she "lived in continual Expectation of Hostilities," afraid the British would attack all along the coast. Her husband applauded her for sustaining "with so much fortitude, the Shocks and terrors of the times. You are really brave, my dear, you are an Heroine." But the attack never came. General Washington arrived in July to take command of the ragtag Continental Army. When he stopped to visit Abigail in Braintree, she found him most impressive.

George Washington, seen here leading his troops into the Battle of Princeton on December 26, 1776, was a daring commander in chief of the Continental Army.

In August, the Congress adjourned briefly, and John was able to slip home for just two weeks to see his delighted family. He could not stay long, however, because Adams was the busiest man in the Congress. Eloquent, persuasive, and efficient, he would eventually serve on twenty-six committees. The questions before Congress were many and urgent. How could the colonies enlist the help of France? Should they outfit armed vessels to attack British ships? And—most important—should the thirteen colonies declare independence from Great Britain?

As soon as Adams had left, the area around Boston was struck by an outbreak of **dysentery**. "The desolation of War is not so distressing as the Havock made by the pestilence," Abigail reported. "Some poor families are mourning the loss of three, four, and five children. . . ." John's brother and Abigail's mother both died in the epidemic.

The Birthday of the United States

In January 1776, a small pamphlet was published in Philadelphia by a British immigrant named Thomas Paine. *Common Sense* was an attack on the institution of kingship and a fervent call for American independence. "For God's sake," Paine urged, "let us come to a final separation. . . . The birthday of a new world is at hand." The pamphlet eventually sold five hundred thousand copies and exerted enormous influence. "*Common Sense* is working a powerful change in the minds of men," George Washington wrote to a friend.

Adams had long believed that a complete break with Great Britain was the colonies' only realistic choice. For eight months, he led the cause for independence, trying to persuade the reluctant delegates that the time for decision had come. He also began to think about what kind of new government Americans should create. "How few of the human race have ever had an opportunity of choosing a system of government for themselves and their children!" he marveled.

In early March, Abigail herself witnessed the most important event of that winter. Under cover of darkness, Washington ordered cannons placed on the hills overlooking Boston Harbor. The next morning, General Howe realized he was trapped. He agreed not to burn Boston down if Washington would let the British troops leave. On March 17, 1776, Abigail watched as the British fleet sailed away. "I feel very differently at the approach of spring to what I did a month ago," Abigail confided to her far-off husband. "I think the Sun looks brighter, the Birds sing more melodiously. . . ."

She was more eager than ever for news from Philadelphia. "I long to hear that you have declared an independancy," she wrote to John. When he wrote up the laws for a new government, she reminded him, rights should be granted to women. Some men were "tyrants," she said, and women needed protection against abusive husbands and fathers. Men and women should be equals, and men should "give up the harsh title of Master for the more tender and endearing one of Friend."

A page from Thomas Paine's *Common Sense*, a pamphlet published in January 1776 that urged the colonies to unite in military action against British dominance.

24   COMMON SENSE

The Sun never ſhined on a cauſe of greater worth, 'Tis not the affair of a City, a County, a Province or a Kingdom ; but of a Continent—of at leaſt one eight part of the habitable Globe. 'Tis not the concern of a day, a year, or an age ; poſterity are virtually involved in the conteſt, and will be more or leſs affected even to the end of time by the proceedings now. Now is the ſeed-time of Continental union, faith and honor. The leaſt fracture now, will be like a name engraved with the point of a pin on the tender rind of a young oak ; the wound will enlarge with the tree, and poſterity read it in full grown characters.

By referring the matter from argument to arms, a new æra for politics is ſtruck—a new method of thinking hath ariſen. All plans, propoſals, &c. prior to

Adams, though, refused to take her seriously and sent her a joking reply. Abigail was not pleased. "Whilst you are proclaiming peace and good will to men, emancipating all nations, you insist on retaining an absolute power over wives," she answered sharply. She could not remain annoyed long, though, because she missed him too much.

Remember the Ladies

While the Continental Congress was preparing the Declaration of Independence, Abigail wrote her husband a letter suggesting that the new laws uphold the rights of women as well as men:

March 31, 1776

In the new Code of Laws which I suppose it will be necessary for you to make I desire you would Remember the Ladies, and be more generous and favourable to them than your ancestors. Do not put such unlimited power into the hands of the Husbands. Remember all Men would be tyrants if they could. If perticular care and attention is not paid to the Laidies we are determined to foment a Rebelion, and will not hold ourselves bound by any laws in which we have no voice, or Representation.

John sent her the following half-serious reply:

April 14, 1776

As to your extraordinary Code of Laws, I cannot but laugh. We have been told that our Struggle has loosened the bands of Government every where. That Children and Apprentices were disobedient—that schools and Colleges were grown turbulent—that Indians slighted their Guardians and Negroes grew

insolent to their masters. But your Letter was the first intimation that another Tribe more numerous and powerfull than all the rest were grown discontented. . . . Depend upon it, We know better than to repeal our Masculine systems . . . in practice you know We are the subjects. We have only the Name of Masters. . . .

Original "Remember the Ladies" document from Abigail to John on March 31, 1776.

An engraving of Thomas Jefferson, who at Adams's insistence single-handedly penned the first draft of the Declaration of Independence.

On June 7, Richard Henry Lee of Virginia rose and presented a resolution for independence. Adams quickly seconded the motion. A committee, composed of Adams, Benjamin Franklin of Pennsylvania, Thomas Jefferson of Virginia, Roger Sherman of Connecticut, and Robert Livingston of New York, was appointed to write up a declaration. At Adams's insistence, Jefferson would write the draft, and the others would edit it.

On July 2, the delegates voted for independence. The next day, John wrote Abigail that "Yesterday . . . a Resolution was passed without one dissenting Colony that these united Colonies are, and of right ought to be free and independent States. . . ." He told her that from then on, July 2 should be celebrated with "Pomp and Parade, and with Shews, Games, Sports, Guns, Bells, Bonfires and Illuminations. . . ." Yet in the coming years, Independence Day would not be July 2 but July 4, the day declaration was officially accepted.

Barely had independence been declared than the Continental Army lost its first major battle at Long Island, New York, on August 27. "In general, our generals were outgeneralled," Adams commented. George Washington and his disillusioned army were forced to retreat north up Manhattan Island and into White Plains, New York, and then south into New Jersey. For the balance of 1776, the two armies chased each other across New Jersey. On Christmas night, Washington surprised the **Hessian** troops at Trenton and won a surprise victory. Then, he attacked nearby Princeton and routed the British Army again. These two victories provided a much-needed boost to American spirits.

Not being able to bear his separation from his family a moment longer, Adams had rushed back to Braintree in October. He was able to stay only twelve weeks, however, before leaving for the Congress again in January 1777. The following July, Abigail gave birth to a stillborn child. "'Tis almost 14 years since we were united, but not more than half that time we had the happiness of living together," she wrote. "The unfeeling world may consider it in what light they please, I consider it a sacrifice to my country and one of my greatest misfortunes."

When the British invaded Philadelphia in September 1777 and the Congress retreated to the nearby town of York, Adams again made it home for two weeks; then a longer separation awaited. That fall, John Adams was chosen to be one of three American delegates to France, joining Benjamin Franklin and Arthur Lee of Virginia, who were already there.

Abigail wanted to go too, but the Atlantic passage was hazardous, threatened both by winter storms and British ships. Ten-year-old Johnny, they decided, would accompany his father to Europe instead.

Mission to France

The voyage was indeed dangerous. The little ship encountered a ferocious storm and survived an armed encounter with a British merchant ship. Adams narrowly avoided a cannonball that hit right over his head. On April 8, 1778, they arrived in Paris, only to find out that Franklin had already negotiated an alliance between France and the United States.

While Johnny attended a nearby boarding school, his father tried to get used to the French court. Though he had previously described Franklin as "a great and good man," he resented the attention paid to "Bonhomme Richard," as the French called the author of the famous *Poor Richard's Almanac.* Franklin, Adams grumbled, had a "Love of Ease and Dissipation" and rarely paid attention to business. Unfortunately, the plainspoken Yankee also disliked the suave French foreign minister, the Comte de Vergennes, who returned his disdain. Adams's first foray into diplomacy was not going well.

Abigail, meanwhile, was nearly frantic with worry and loneliness. In the nine months since John had departed, she complained, she had received only three brief letters. "By heaven," she asked, "if you could you have changed hearts with some frozen

Benjamin Franklin, depicted here receiving a warm French welcome, was greatly admired by all of France, whereas Adams had a difficult time adjusting to the genteel style of the French diplomats.

Laplander." John was deeply disturbed by her accusations. Surely after all this time she could not doubt his love. "Can Protestations of affection be necessary?" he asked. "I beg you would never write to me in such a strain for it really makes me unhappy."

Then, abruptly, Congress appointed Franklin the only **commissioner** to France and John sailed home again to a very happy reunion. That summer of 1779, Adams performed a great service for his home state by writing the first draft of the Massachusetts Constitution. The first constitution ever written in the history of the world, it greatly influenced the U.S. Constitution, composed eight years later.

The close happy family days would not last, however. In November, Adams was once again called on by his country to travel to France to begin the peace negotiations with Great Britain. Abigail was deeply disturbed by the prospect of another parting, yet she would never have asked her husband not to go. She understood and encouraged his hunger for fame. "For myself," she wrote, "I have little ambition or pride—for my husband, I freely own I have much."

Her sense of sacrifice was increased by the departure of both twelve-year-old Johnny and nine-year-old Charles, who would accompany their father to Paris. John thought his growing sons needed a father's guidance and would benefit from a European education. After just two years, Charles would become ill and homesick for his mother and sail home by himself. Abigail would be separated from her husband and oldest son, however, for a long and dreary five years.

Though Adams's mission to France was a hopeful one, the Revolutionary War was not over yet. On May 12, 1780, came the most devastating defeat of the war, when American troops lost the Battle of Charleston, in South Carolina, to British general Charles Cornwallis. "Our present situation is very disagreable," Abigail wrote her husband darkly.

John was not having a successful time either, once again having difficulty with the Comte de Vergennes. Vergennes actually wrote a complaining letter about Adams to Franklin, who sent it on to the Congress. Mortified, Adams left France and traveled to Holland. There, he hoped to raise some money for the American cause. Abigail heard from neither John nor her son for more than a year. "I am," she wrote, "much afflicted with a disorder called the *Heartache*." In Amsterdam, John fell deathly ill.

Finally came the welcome news: General George Washington and his Continental Army had defeated the British at Yorktown, Virginia, on October 19, 1781. The following year Adams became Ambassador to the Netherlands and obtained a much-needed Dutch loan to the United States before being summoned back to Paris to work on the peace negotiations.

As the bargaining dragged on, John and Abigail debated what to do. Should he come home or should she meet him in Paris? On their eighteenth wedding anniversary, Abigail wrote her absent husband a poignant letter. "Who shall give me back Time?" she asked. ". . . Those years I cannot recall?" Not until September 3, 1783, was the Treaty of Paris ending the Revolutionary War formally signed. Adams promptly fell ill again. "I must go to you or you must come to me," he wrote in despair. "I cannot live in this horrid Solitude!"

Abigail agreed. In spring, she would hasten to her "dearest friend."

This image depicts the surrender of General Cornwallis to General Washington at Yorktown on October 19, 1781. However, the encounter never took place. Claiming illness, Cornwallis sent his second-in-command in his stead, and Washington, in response, did the same.

A NEW NATION

Abigail and nineteen-year-old Nabby set sail for Europe on June 20, 1784, leaving Thomas and Charles to stay with Abigail's sister Elizabeth in Braintree. It was a rough, uncomfortable journey. "Every thing wet, dirty, and cold, ourselves Sick," Abigail grumbled after a bad storm.

Yet it was worth it. Shortly after they arrived in London, a tall, distinguished-looking young man entered their hotel room. "Oh my mama and my dear sister!" he cried out, rushing into their arms. It was seventeen-year-old John Quincy, sent ahead by his father, who was detained in the Netherlands.

A week later came the day they had long been praying for. One day when she returned to the hotel, Nabby found an unknown hat and cane in the front parlor. She ran upstairs, and her father greeted her "with all the tenderness of an affectionate parent after so long an absence." Abigail left no record of her first reunion with her dearest friend. "Poets and painters wisely draw a veil over those scenes which surpass the pen of the one and the pencil of the other" she wrote her sister Mary. "We were indeed a very happy family once more."

The reunited family traveled to Paris, where they rented a large, elegant house in the suburbs. Abigail alternately disapproved of and was fascinated by a city in which "the business of life [is] . . . pleasure." At the ballet, she wrote her sister in amazement, the girls sprang "two feet from the floor . . . and as perfectly showing their garters and drawers as though no petticoat had been worn." Yet after Abigail recovered from her initial shock, she had to admit the ballet was beautiful.

Paris gave John Adams the chance to renew his friendship with Thomas Jefferson, who, with Adams, was charged with negotiating

The young John Quincy Adams in a pastel by Isaak Schmidt, 1783. After spending years separated by an ocean, Abigail was finally reunited with her son.

The Adams family settled into their new home in Auteuil, near Paris. At first overwhelmed in the forty-room house, Abigail later grew to love its elegance and "delightful" garden.

commercial treaties with European countries. Abigail formed an instant friendship with the charming, intellectual Virginian. In May 1785 came word that the Congress had appointed Jefferson the new ambassador to France. "I shall really regret to leave Mr. Jefferson," Abigail confided to her sister Mary. "[He is] one of the choice ones of the Earth."

American Ambassadors

To Adams's intense satisfaction, he himself had been named minister to the Court of St. James—the first American ambassador to Great Britain. While Abigail busied herself with the move, John composed his introductory address to King George III. On June 1, 1785, he arrived at St. James's Palace in London for his private audience.

"I shall esteem myself the happiest of men," Adams told the king, "if I can be instrumental in recommending my country more and more to your Majesty's royal benevolence, and of restoring . . . the old good nature and the old good humor between people who, though separated by an ocean and under different governments, have the same language, a similar religion, and kindred blood."

King George seemed much moved by the meeting, and Adams hoped that his ministry would proceed well. The British were hardly prepared, however, to treat the upstart American as an equal.

George III, king of England. Although the king treated the new ambassador from the United States courteously, John and Abigail Adams received a cool reception from the rest of British society. Engraving from a painting by Benjamin West, 1778.

"An ambassador from America!" jeered a London newspaper. "Good heavens what a sound!" Adams's primary task was to try to negotiate a treaty to open British ports and also to get rid of some remaining British forts in the United States. The new nation was poor and weak and had little bargaining power, however, and Adams felt that he enjoyed minimal success.

Abigail tried to accustom herself to court life. She really did enjoy the London theater, seeing for the first time the Shakespearean plays she had loved as a girl. One night, she joked, she saw a "learned pig, dancing dogs, and a little hare that beats a drum." The most important family event to take place in London was the marriage of Nabby to Adams's aide, William Stephens Smith, in 1786. Within a year, John and Abigail were the proud grandparents of a little boy. By that point, all three Adams sons were attending Harvard, from which John Quincy graduated in 1787.

In the Adamses' absence, the Constitutional Convention was taking place back in Philadelphia. A new government was being formed, and Adams wanted to be part of it. In 1788, Congress recalled him to the United States, praising the "patriotism, perseverance, integrity, and diligence with which [he] had ably and faithfully served his country."

To their surprise and delight, John and Abigail Adams returned to a grand welcome. When their ship sailed into Boston Harbor on June 17, 1788, church bells pealed, cannons boomed, and more than a thousand citizens lined the wharf to cheer them home. They settled quickly into a new seven-room house in Braintree they named Peacefield. They would not be there long, however.

The nation's first presidential election was held the next spring. Each elector in the **electoral college** would cast two votes; the winner would be the president, and the runner-up would be vice president. Everyone knew the first president would be George Washington, who was indeed elected unanimously. And the first vice president of the United States, with 34 out of 69 votes, would be—John Adams!

At the Seat of Government

John left for the new capital, New York City, where he was sworn in during a quiet ceremony on April 21, 1789. A week later, he attended George Washington's **inauguration**.

Unfortunately, Adams would find his new job disappointing and frustrating. Though he was eager to serve his country and aid his president, he soon found that as vice president he had not "the smallest degree of power to do any good either in the executive, legislative, [or] judicial departments," as he wrote a friend. Even though Adams was president of the Senate, he could not debate laws, merely vote in the case of a tie.

At the first meeting of the Senate, Adams brought up the question of the president's title. With his approval, elaborate titles such as "His Elective Highness" or "His Highness the President of the United States and Protector of Rights of the Same," were suggested. When word of the debate got out, critics suggested that the new vice president might be a secret monarchist. Perhaps John himself should be dubbed "His Rotundity," Senator Ralph Izard sneered. Finally the plain title of "Mr. President" was chosen, to Washington's relief.

George Washington's inauguration at Federal Hall, New York, April 30, 1789. Illustration by Howard Pyle.

Abigail arrived in June and settled into a New York country house at Richmond Hill with a magnificent view. Her primary task as the vice president's wife was to fulfill her social obligations —making and returning social calls and hosting dinner parties. At Martha Washington's levees, or receptions, Abigail stood on her right side. She much admired Mrs. Washington, and they soon became good friends. "She is plain in dress, but that plainness is the best of every article," Abigail told her sister Mary. "Her hair is white, her teeth beautiful." George Washington, Abigail correctly judged, was perhaps the only man who could hold the new **republic** together. "He is polite with dignity," she wrote, "affable without formality, distant without haughtiness . . . modest, wise, and good."

A map of the city of Washington, D.C., showing Pierre L'Enfant's 1792 plan for the new permanent seat of government.

Abigail enjoyed living in New York, where she was close to her daughter Nabby and her family and to her son Charles, who was just starting a law practice. Yet in July 1790, she discovered that the capital was being moved to Philadelphia for ten years and then to a permanent home on the Potomac River, on land taken from both Virginia and Maryland. Once again she had to pack all their furniture and household goods and move to an unfinished house in Philadelphia.

John and Abigail's family was a constant worry. Nabby, who now had three children, was married to a man who could not support her. She was unhappy and disillusioned, uncertain what the future would bring. Charles, charming and lovable, had developed a liking for strong drink at Harvard, and was, Abigail said, "not at peace with himself." Brilliant John Quincy, who had recently established a law practice in Boston, was lonely and depressed. Even Abigail was not well. In the summer of 1791, she fell ill with **malaria**, which she would get recurrently for many years to follow.

The news from abroad was unsettling, too. In 1789, the French Revolution resulted in the overthrow of the French **monarchy** and the spread of violence and chaos across Europe. Adams immediately began writing a series of anonymous articles expressing his view that this revolution would lead to more brutality and lawlessness. The French people, he thought, could no more create a democracy through violence than "a snowball can exist in the streets of Philadelphia under a burning Sun." His old friend Thomas Jefferson, however, cheered the revolutionaries on. "Half the earth [could be] devastated," he wrote, if it would ensure the "liberty of the whole."

Across Europe, other nations went to war against France. Jefferson's pro-French political party, called the Democratic-Republicans, urged the United States to aid France, which had stood by the colonies in the American Revolution. Washington and Adams, however, understood that the infant nation was in no position, militarily or financially, to risk a war.

In 1792, Adams made the decision to run for reelection as vice president. Although he denigrated his job as "the most insignificant office that ever the Invention of man contrived," he was loyal to Washington and interested in remaining in politics. In the fall of 1792, both were reelected. Abigail, however, would not be returning to Philadelphia. Weakened by relapses of malaria and eager to devote herself full time to family and finances, she elected to live at Braintree, now renamed Quincy in honor of her great-grandfather, John Quincy.

Once again, John and Abigail were apart for six months at a time. In her chatty letters, Abigail kept her husband informed about everyday matters on the farm. "I want to sit down and converse with you, every evening I sit here alone," she wrote him. She told him about buying cows, and nursing a sick lamb, and defending a young black boy who wanted to go to school. John repeated how much he missed her. "I am as impatient to see you as I used to be twenty years ago," he declared.

John Quincy Adams, who as a teen had accompanied his father John on his diplomatic mission to France, was appointed ambassador to the Netherlands at the age of twenty-seven.

She assured him of her continuing devotion. "Years subdue the ardor of passion," she wrote, "but in lieu thereof a Friendship and affection deep rooted subsists which defies the ravages of Time."

John chided her not to talk about age. "If I were near, I would soon convince you that I am not above forty," he wrote.

They were pleased when twenty-seven-year-old John Quincy was appointed ambassador to the Netherlands. Abigail had always been convinced that "The Time will come when this Young Man will be sought for as a jewel of great price."

In 1793, Washington issued the Neutrality Proclamation, which stated that the United States would not take sides in the European wars. As a result, Washington and other **Federalists** were subjected to a barrage of criticism. Because the British were seizing American ships and preventing trade with France, many Americans supported direct retaliation. The outcry grew louder when Washington dispatched Chief Justice John Jay to Britain to negotiate a treaty. Though Jay's Treaty prevented another war with Britain, it did not prohibit the British from continuing to capture American ships and force American sailors into naval service. Democratic-Republicans charged that Washington had caved in to the British government.

A Glorious Reward

Tired and discouraged, Washington decided not to run for a third term. Adams then had an important decision to make: Should he run for president himself? "Either we must enter upon Ardours more trying than ever yet experienced," he told Abigail, "or retire to Quincy, Farmers for Life."

The presidency was indeed a "most unpleasant seat, full of thorns, briars, thistles," Abigail wrote back. Yet, she went on, the presidency would be a "flattering and Glorious reward" for his years of service.

In the election of 1796, Adams's opponent was Thomas Jefferson. As was the tradition at the time, Adams and Jefferson both stayed home while their supporters campaigned. It was a bitter and hateful campaign. Alexander Hamilton, leader of the Federalists, called Jefferson a French-loving coward and atheist. The Democratic-Republicans retorted that Adams was an old, fat, pro-British monarchist.

On February 8, 1797, it fell to John Adams as leader of the Senate to open the envelope containing the ballots from the electoral college. He had received 71 votes to Thomas Jefferson's 68. As first runner-up, Jefferson would automatically become vice president. John Adams would be the next president of the United States.

The French Revolution

On July 14, 1789, a mob of peasants and **radicals** stormed the Bastille, an ancient royal prison in Paris. This act signaled the beginning of the French Revolution and the overthrow of the hereditary Bourbon family monarchy. **Liberals** throughout Europe and the United States were inspired by the slogan of the Revolution—*Liberté Egalitié, Fraternité* (Liberty, Equality, Fraternity)—and applauded the establishment of a republic. However, when other European monarchies sent their armies into France to support King Louis XVI, radicals seized power, and the country degenerated into the Reign of Terror. From 1793 to 1794, massacres and executions resulted in the deaths of more than ten thousand people, including the king and his wife, Marie Antoinette. Aided by a brilliant young general named Napoleon Bonaparte, France fought against an alliance of Great Britain, the Netherlands, Austria, and Prussia. Napoleon became **dictator** of France in 1800 and continued the military campaign that plunged Europe into fifteen more years of war.

CHAPTER SIX

MR. AND MRS. PRESIDENT

O n March 4, 1797, John Adams put on his pearl gray suit and ceremonial sword and went to Congress Hall in Philadelphia, where he was sworn in as the second president of the United States. "A solemn scene it was indeed, and it was made more affecting to me by the presence of the General [Washington], whose countenance was as serene and unclouded as the day," John reported to Abigail. "Methought I heard him say, 'Ay! I am fairly out and you fairly in! See which of us will be happiest.'" No other member of the Adams family was present. Abigail, still in Quincy, was keeping vigil by the bedside of her husband's dying mother. Soon John was begging her to come back to Philadelphia. "I never wanted your advice and assistance more in my life," he told her. In another letter he wrote, "The times are critical and dangerous, and I must have you here to assist me."

John Adams in a presidential portrait by Peter S. Duval.

War Fever

It would be a difficult presidency. For the first and only time in American history, the vice president belonged to a different political party from the president's, and Adams knew he could not count on Jefferson's support for his programs or decisions. As events would prove, Adams could not count on the backing of his own party, either.

He soon felt the lack. In 1797, the French, angry about the Jay Treaty, began to seize American ships. Furious Federalists called for war with France, but Adams knew that the United States, with no navy or standing army, was not strong enough to go to war with anyone. Instead, he sent a delegation to Paris to discuss neutrality. Month after month went by, and he heard nothing. Finally, two of his commissioners, John Marshall and Charles Cotesworth Pinckney, came home with a message from the French foreign minister, Charles-Maurice de Talleyrand-Périgord.

To his rising indignation, Adams found out that Talleyrand had sent three secret agents—known as *X*, *Y*, and *Z*—to deal with the Americans before France would agree to start negotiations. The agents demanded a bribe: $250,000 for Talleyrand himself and a $10 million loan to France. "No! No! Not a sixpence!" the outraged Pinckney had replied.

When the XYZ Affair became public knowledge in the United States, it caused a national outcry: "Millions for defense, but not one cent for tribute!" With public sentiment on the side of war, Adams took the opportunity to build up the U.S. military. He created the Department of the Navy and ordered the construction of battleships, including the USS *Constitution*, later nicknamed Old Ironsides. In addition, a ten-thousand-soldier army was called up. General Washington put on his old uniform and prepared to lead the new army. At Washington's insistence, his previous **aide-de-camp,** Alexander Hamilton, was made the inspector general, the second in command. That meant that if war were to be declared with France, Hamilton would be the acting head of the army. During the Quasi-War, or undeclared war, that ensued, America captured eighty French ships in the West Indies.

A 1798 British cartoon pokes fun at the tense relations between the United States and France after the XYZ Affair. Five Frenchman plunder a woman, representing the United States, as the rest of Europe, represented by five figures in the distance, look on.

Troubled Times

In the midst of war fever, ultra-**conservative** Federalists in Congress passed the Alien and Sedition Acts. The Alien Acts, aimed at foreigners, allowed the president to deport any foreigners he thought were a threat to the country. It also increased the number of years it took for newcomers to become citizens from five to fourteen years. Immigrants, Federalists knew, usually voted for the civic-minded Democratic-Republican Party. They used these acts to block immigrant votes.

The Sedition Act said that anyone who criticized the government could be fined or jailed. It was in clear defiance of the First Amendment to the Constitution, which guaranteed freedom of speech, including freedom of the press. Abigail, who had seen her husband criticized as "old, querulous, bald, blind, crippled, [and] toothless," strongly supported the Sedition Act. She hoped it would silence the Democratic-Republican press. Thomas Jefferson warned that the laws undercut basic American rights.

Although Adams was not the author of the Alien and Sedition Acts, he did sign them. He lived to regret it. Most historians agree that they were the low point of his presidency.

In preparation for war, Adams's Federalist Party passed a series of controversial Alien and Sedition Acts that were met by violent protest from Democratic-Republicans. A 1798 etching depicts Vermont Democratic-Republican Congressman Matthew Lyon attacking a Federalist opponent on the floor of Congress.

In summer 1798, John and Abigail went back home to Peacefield for what Abigail hoped would be a relaxing summer break. Almost immediately, she fell desperately ill and came close to dying from a combination of dysentery and fever. John was forced to return to Philadelphia alone in November.

Adams felt worn and tired during that cold winter of 1799. "I am Old, Old, very Old and never shall be very well—certainly while in this office," he lamented. All alone, with the country on the verge of a war with France, he had a decision to make. He still wished to avoid a conflict and waited for some sign from the French government. He got it when his son Thomas, who had been with John Quincy, in Europe, returned with a letter from Talleyrand. It informed the president that any commissioners the United States might send to France would be met "with the respect due to the representative of a free, independent, and powerful country." It was clearly not the message of a man eager for war.

On February 18, 1799, Adams sent a note to Congress informing them that he was sending another envoy to France to seek peace. The High Federalists, thunderstruck, were furious. When another coup upset the existing French government, Adams delayed sending the envoys. Hamilton took advantage of the delay to make one last plea. Vehemently, he told Adams that Britain was assured of ultimate victory against France and would restore France's Bourbon monarchy to the throne. Adams listened to him calmly and then ordered the envoys to set sail for France in November.

In September 1799, Adams found out that Charles, bankrupt and an alcoholic, had deserted his wife and children. Adams was so disturbed that he renounced his son then and there, vowing never to see him again. Abigail was more charitable. She visited Charles when he returned to his family, terribly ill.

The Democratic-Republicans v the Federalists

When George Washington took office in 1789, the United States had no political parties. Eight years later, the nation was divided into two rival groups that distrusted and disliked each other. Washington's secretary of state Thomas Jefferson led the Democratic-Republicans (later called the Democrats), which attracted small farmers, especially in the West and South; craftspeople; and recent immigrants. The party stood for strong state government, agricultural interests, and the civil rights of ordinary people. Washington's secretary of the treasury, Alexander Hamilton, became the leader of the Federalist Party, which attracted Northern lawyers, merchants, and manufacturers as well as wealthy planters. The Federalists stood for a strong central government, support for industry, banking, shipping and trade, and leadership by a small influential set.

When the French Revolution plunged Europe into war, Democratic-Republicans argued that the United States should support France and the Federalists wanted to strengthen ties with Great Britain. Even after John Adams became president, Hamilton continued to lead the most extreme anti-French and pro-British Federalists, called the High Federalists. When Adams, a political moderate, refused to declare war on France, Hamilton turned against him in the election of 1800.

"All is lost," she said sadly. "Ruin and destruction swallowed him up."

During the winter and spring of 1800, Adams waited to hear the results of his peace mission to France. With the rest of the government, he prepared to move to Washington City, the new, half-finished collection of buildings on the Potomac River. On November 1, 1800, President Adams pulled up in a coach and gazed at the stately President's House, the largest home in America.

When Abigail arrived two weeks later, she found the President's House still damp with paint and fresh plaster. She used the huge east audience room to hang her wet laundry.

Benjamin Henry Latrobe's 1807 proposal for alterations of the President's House in Washington. When the Adamses moved into the building in 1800, it was not yet known as the "White House."

Farewell to Politics

At the beginning of fall 1800, John Adams believed he still had a chance to win the upcoming election. The Democratic-Republicans had nominated Jefferson for president and Aaron Burr of New York for vice president. Federalist supporters praised Adams as "a good husband, a good father, a good citizen, and a good man," but then Hamilton struck. In a pamphlet, Hamilton attacked him for his "great intrinsic defects of Character," "ungovernable temper," and "disgusting egotism." Immediately Adams realized that by splitting the Federalist vote, Hamilton had lost him the election.

The very day that the electors met to cast their votes in early December, 1800, John and Abigail found out that their son Charles, only thirty years old, had died. A few days later, the news came that Adams had, indeed, lost the race for president.

No one truly knew who had won the election, however. Jefferson had 73 votes; Adams had 65; and surprisingly, Aaron Burr also had 73. The House of Representatives voted 35 times before the tie between Jefferson and Burr was broken. Convinced that the election of Burr would be a disaster for the country, Alexander Hamilton persuaded his supporters to vote for his long-time rival, Jefferson. Thomas Jefferson would be the third president of the United States.

Adams had just two months remaining in office. He learned to his great satisfaction that a peace treaty had been signed in Paris on October 3. It was, he felt, his finest accomplishment. Years later, he would ask for his tombstone to read, "Here lies John Adams, who took upon himself the responsibility of peace with France in the year 1800."

Thomas Jefferson defeated Adams in the election of 1800 that divided the country in a bitter contest between Federalists and Democratic-Republicans.

Also, when Congress passed the Judiciary Act on February 13, he used the remaining few weeks to reward friends and family with appointments on the federal court. Most important, he appointed John Marshall Chief Justice of the Supreme Court. Later, Democratic-Republicans accused Adams of staying up until midnight appointing his "midnight judges," but Adams said, "My conscience is as clear as a Crystal glass."

When he left office, Adams was a disappointed man. Still, he was proud of his accomplishments as president. He had left his nation, he wrote, "with its coffers full" and with "fair prospects of peace with all the world, its commerce flourishing, its navy glorious, its agriculture uncommonly productive and lucrative."

At four o'clock in the morning on Inauguration Day, March 4, 1801, John and Abigail Adams left Washington City and started on the long road back to Quincy. Their days on the public stage were over.

FARMERS FOR LIFE

After twenty-six years in politics, "Farmer John," as Adams called himself, was home on the farm. The transition was too abrupt, and Adams was upset, sometimes bitter, about his difficult presidency and rejection by American voters. "If I were to go over my Life again, I would be a Shoemaker rather than an American Statesman," he growled in a moment of self-pity.

Abigail settled more easily into the rural life. By then, the Adamses owned three farms, 600 acres (about 243 ha) in all. "I have commenced my operation of a dairy woman," she wrote her son-in-law Colonel William Smith. "[Nabby] might see me at five o'clock in the morning skimming my milk." In addition, there was family to take care of. John and Abigail had taken in Charles's wife, Sally, and their two daughters, and Nabby and her four children visited often. For five years, Thomas, his wife Nancy, and their children lived with his parents as well, before moving back to the old Adams homestead in Quincy.

Most exciting, after seven years abroad, John Quincy Adams, his new wife Louisa Catherine Adams, and their son George Washington Adams returned from Europe, where John Quincy had been ambassador to the Netherlands and then Prussia. John and Abigail were very proud of John Quincy, the most successful of their children. When his diplomatic career once again took him abroad in 1809, they missed him dreadfully.

Nabby's story was a much sadder one. In 1811, she fell ill with breast cancer and had a **mastectomy**, without anesthetics, in the Adams home. After a prolonged recuperation, she seemed to be on the mend, yet the cancer had spread, and two years later she came home again to die. "The loss is irreparable," Abigail wrote to John Quincy in Russia. The Adamses' love and their faith in God enabled them to bear up, however. There were blessings still left, Abigail assured her son. Chief among them were "the life, health, and cheerfulness of your father."

Farewell to Old Friends

After four years at home, Adams renewed a correspondence with one of his old friends from the Revolution, Dr. Benjamin Rush, who, in turn, urged him to write to his old friend and adversary Thomas Jefferson. The two patriots were "the North and South poles of the American Revolution," Rush wrote to Adams. "Some talked, some wrote, and some fought to promote and establish it, but you and Mr. Jefferson *thought* for us all." On New Year's Day, 1812, Adams took up his pen to follow Rush's advice. Thus began one of the most astonishing correspondences in American history.

A current photo of the Adams house in Quincy, Massachusetts, where John returned after his disappointing defeat in 1800.

At home in Charlottesville, Virginia, Jefferson was glad to hear from Adams. "A letter from you calls up recollections very dear to my mind," he said. "It carried me back to the times when, beset with difficulties and dangers, we were fellow laborers in the same cause, struggling for what is most valuable to man, his right of self-government." Though they never met again, for the next fifteen years, Adams and Jefferson discussed politics, philosophy, religion, old friends, and the Revolution.

Abigail, too, never lost her lively mind. "At the age of seventy," she admitted, "I feel more interest in all that's done beneath the circuit of the sun than some others do at—What shall I say, 35 or 40?"

Old age was overtaking them, though. In the fall of 1818, Abigail fell ill with **typhoid fever**. Soon it became apparent that this was to be her last illness. Adams wrote a dispairing letter to Thomas Jefferson: "The dear partner of my life for fifty-four years as a Wife and for many years more as a Lover, now lies in extremis, forbidden to speak or be spoken to." On October 28, Abigail Adams slipped away at age seventy-four.

John Quincy Adams

John Quincy Adams served his country faithfully for fifty-three years. His diplomatic career began in 1794 when George Washington appointed him as minister to the Netherlands. In later years, he served as minister to Prussia (1797), U.S. senator (1803), minister to Russia (1809), peace commissioner after the War of 1812, minister to England (1815), and secretary of state (1817).

In 1824, Adams ran for president against war hero

Following in his father's footsteps, John Quincy Adams was elected sixth president of the United States in 1824.

Andrew Jackson of Tennessee and Henry Clay of Kentucky. When Adams came in second to Jackson in the popular and electoral vote, Clay threw his votes to Adams, thus securing him the presidency. A few days later, after Adams nominated Clay as his secretary of state, Jackson's supporters sneered that he had made a "corrupt bargain." Adams proved to be a largely unpopular and unsuccessful president. His grumpy disposition and inflexible views made it difficult for him to retain political allies and work with Congress.

After losing the 1828 election to Jackson, John Quincy Adams became the only former U.S. president ever to serve in the House of Representatives. In Congress, he found the cause that possessed him for the rest of his life—the fight against slavery.

John Quincy Adams collapsed at his desk in the House of Representatives and died on February 21, 1848.

Even in his final years, Adams maintained an avid correspondence with his friend Thomas Jefferson.

Grief-stricken as he was, John rallied. For the next eight years, he continued to enjoy his farm, his grandchildren, and his books. His greatest regret, he said in 1824, was that John Quincy's proud mother had not lived to see her son become the sixth president of the United States.

The fiftieth anniversary of the Declaration of Independence, July 4, 1826, was fast approaching. Adams and Jefferson were the last signers still alive, and they were both determined to hang on for the celebrations. When a delegation asked Adams for some suitable words for the occasion, the feeble old man could manage only two: "Independence forever!"

On the day of the anniversary, Adams was sinking rapidly. Late in the afternoon he rallied and whispered, "Thomas Jefferson survives!" In fact, Jefferson had died earlier, at about 1 P.M. At 6:20 P.M. that evening, July 4, 1826, ninety-one-year-old John Adams, too, breathed his last.

1735	John Adams is born on October 30
1744	Abigail Smith is born on November 22
1755	John graduates from Harvard College in July
1764	Abigail and John marry on October 25
1765	Abigail (Nabby) Adams is born on July 14; Stamp Act is passed
1767	John Quincy Adams is born on July 11
1768	Susanna Adams is born on December 28
1770	Susanna Adams dies on February 4; Boston Massacre occurs on March 5; Charles Adams is born on May 29
1772	Thomas Boylston Adams is born on September 15
1773	Boston Tea Party occurs on December 16
1774	John becomes delegate to First Continental Congress on September 5
1775	First shots of the Revolutionary War are fired at Lexington and Concord on April 19; John becomes delegate to Second Continental Congress on May 10
1776	British forces are driven out of Boston on March 17; Declaration of Independence is signed on July 4
1777	Elizabeth Adams is stillborn on July 11
1778	John and John Quincy sail for France on February 14
1779	John and John Quincy return from Europe on August 3; John, John Quincy, and Charles sail for France on November 15
1782	John is appointed first American ambassador to the Netherlands
1783	The Treaty of Paris ends the Revolutionary War on September 3
1784	Abigail and Nabby sail for Europe on June 20
1785	John is appointed first ambassador to Great Britain on February 24
1787	Constitutional Convention begins May 25
1788	The Adamses return to the United States on June 17
1789	John takes the oath of office for vice president of the United States on April 21
1793	John is inaugurated vice president for a second term
1797	John becomes president of the United States on March 4; XYZ Affair occurs
1798	Adams signs the Alien and Sedition Acts
1800	A Treaty with France is signed on October 3; John and Abigail move into the new President's House in Washington, D.C. in November; Adams loses the election for a second term in December
1818	Abigail Adams dies on October 28
1825	John Quincy Adams is inaugurated president of the United States on March 4
1826	John Adams dies on July 4

GLOSSARY

aide-de-camp—a military assistant.

boycott—to refuse to buy or use goods or services in order to make a protest or bring about change.

commercial treaty—a formal agreement that governs the buying and selling of goods or services between two or more nations.

commissioner—a government representative.

conservative—a viewpoint that supports established values or institutions and does not favor taking chances or risks.

Continental Congress—the gathering of representatives from American colonies that met between 1774 and the end of the Revolutionary War. It adopted both the Declaration of Independence and the Articles of Confederation.

dame school—a school for young children taught by a woman with no formal training, usually in her own house.

delegates—representatives to a convention or conference.

dictator—a ruler who has total authority.

dysentery—an infectious disease of the intestines causing severe pain and diarrhea.

electoral college—group of people from each state that votes for the President of the United States based on the popular vote in each state.

Federalists—political party that supported a strong central government and favored aiding Great Britain.

garrison—a military post, such as a fort, where troops are stationed.

Hessian—German soldiers who fought on the side of the British during the American Revolution.

inauguration—a ceremony at which a public official, especially a president, is sworn into office.

liberals—people who favor progress and change in government.

malaria—a disease carried by mosquitoes that causes chills, fever, and sweating.

martial law—the establishment of military control over a region.

mastectomy—the removal of a woman's breast by surgery.

militia—a group of trained citizens who serve as soldiers in an emergency.

minutemen—volunteers trained to fight the British on a moment's notice.

monarchy—a nation or government ruled by a ruler such as a king, queen, or emperor.

Parliament—the legislative body of Britain, made up of the House of Commons and House of Lords.

Puritan—a member of a group of Protestants in England in the 1500s and 1600s who believed in simpler forms of worship. Some Puritans settled in what is now Massachusetts.

quarantine—the keeping of a person or animal away from others to stop a disease from spreading.

radical—someone who supports extreme social and political change.

republic—a nation in which citizens elect representatives to govern them.

saltbox—a style of house with two stories in the front and a roof that slants down over one rear story.

smallpox—a contagious viral disease characterized by a fever and pus-filled pimples that often leave scars.

typhoid fever—a bacterial disease that is characterized by high fever, diarrhea, and swelling of the intestines and is spread through infected food or water.

Further Reading

Adkins, Jan. *John Adams: Young Revolutionary.* (Childhood of Famous Americans). New York: Aladdin Paperbacks, 2002.

Bober, Natalie S. *Abigail Adams: Witness to a Revolution.* New York: Simon Pulse, 1998.

Bober, Natalie S. *Countdown to Independence.* New York: Atheneum, 2001.

Burgan, Michael and Meier Schlesinger. *John Adams: Second U.S. President.* (Revolutionary War Leaders). White Plains, NY: Chelsea House Publications, 2000.

Davis, Kate. *Abigail Adams.* (Revolutionary War Leaders). Woodbridge, CT: Blackbirch Press, 2002.

Feinberg, Barbara Silberdick. *John Adams: America's Second President.* New York: Children's Press, 2003.

Gormley, Beatrice. *First Ladies: Women Who Called the White House Home.* Madison, WI: Turtleback Books, 2004.

Harness, Cheryl. *The Revolutionary John Adams.* Washington, D.C.: National Geographic Society, 2003.

Lukes, Bonnie L. *John Adams: Public Servant.* (Notable Americans). Greensboro, NC: Morgan Reynolds Publishing, 2000.

Mayo, Edith P. (ed.) *The Smithsonian Book of First Ladies: Their Lives, Times, and Issues.* New York: Henry Holt/Smithsonian Institution, 1996.

McCollum, Sean. *John Quincy Adams.* New York: Children's Press, 2003.

McPherson, Stephanie Sammartino. *My Dear Husband: Important Letters of Abigail Adams.* (Great Moments in American History). New York: Rosen Publishing Group, 2003.

Rinaldi, Ann. *Fifth of March: A Story of the Boston Massacre.* New York: Gulliver, 2004.

St. George, Judith. *John & Abigail Adams: An American Love Story.* New York: Holiday House, 2001.

FURTHER INFORMATION

Places to Visit

Abigail Adams Birthplace
180 Norton Street
Weymouth, MA 02188
(781) 335-4205

Adams National Historical Park
1250 Hancock Street
Quincy, MA 02169
(617) 770-1175

The Freedom Trail
Visitors Information Center
147 Tremont Street
Boston Common
Boston, MA 02111
(617) 242-5642

The National First Ladies' Library
Education and Research Center
205 Market Avenue South
Canton, OH 44702
(330) 452-0876

White House
1600 Pennsylvania Avenue, N.W.
Washington, D.C. 20500
(202) 456-2121

USS *Constitution* Museum
Building 22
Boston National Historical Park
Charlestown Navy Yard
Boston, MA 02129
(617) 426-1812

Web Sites

The Abigail Adams Historical Society
www.abigailadams.org

Adams National Historical Park
www.nps.gov/adam/

The Adams Papers
Massachusetts Historical Society
www.masshist.org/adams.html

Boston National Historical Park
www.nps.gov/bost/

The First Ladies of the United States
of America
www.whitehouse.gov

The Freedom Trail
www.thefreedomtrail.org

Internet Public Library, Presidents of
the United States (IPL POTUS)
www.ipl.org/div/potus/jadams.html

The National First Ladies' Library
www.firstladies.org

INDEX

Page numbers in **bold** represent photographs.

About the Author

Ruth Ashby has written many award-winning biographies and nonfiction books for children, including *Herstory*, *The Elizabethan Age*, and *Pteranodon: The Life Story of a Pterosaur*. She lives on Long Island with her husband, daughter, and dog, Nubby.